ROBERT L. HUNTER

HELPING
WHEN IT HURTS

A
Practical Guide
to Helping Relationships

FORTRESS PRESS   PHILADELPHIA

All Scripture quotations in this publication are from the Holy
Bible, New International Version, Copyright © 1973, 1978,
1984, International Bible Society.

COPYRIGHT © 1985 BY FORTRESS PRESS

All rights reserved. No part of this publication may be repro-
duced, stored in a retrieval system, or transmitted in any form
or by any means, electronic, mechanical, photocopying, record-
ing, or otherwise, without the prior permission of the copyright
owner.

Library of Congress Cataloging in Publication Data

Hunter, Robert L.
  Helping when it hurts.

  Bibliography: p.
  1. Helping behavior—Religious aspects—Christianity.
2. Pastoral psychology. 3. Peer counseling in the church.
I. Title.
BV4012.2.H835 1985   248   85-47738
ISBN 0-8006-1879-3

Printed in the United States of America   1-1879

95 94 93 92 91   5 6 7 8 9 10

To my parents
John and Amy Hunter
who taught me how to care.

CONTENTS

ACKNOWLEDGMENTS

Many friends have contributed invaluable suggestions and guidance in the preparation of the final text of this manuscript. Without their assistance and encouragement, the completion of the project would have been all but impossible.

My deepest gratitude is due to Beth Crozier, Shari Wann, and Marjie Williams, whose painstaking work on various stages of the manuscript helped to overcome many of its inadequacies. Jean McDonald and Vicki Williams were most helpful with typing and retyping parts of the manuscript. Harley Bierce gave invaluable encouragement and suggestions from start to finish.

INTRODUCTION

When someone you know goes through a serious crisis or loss, it is natural for you to feel helpless. Whether that crisis relates to a broken relationship, desertion by a husband or wife, the death of a family member, illness, or injury, the effects may devastate those who experience it. If you care about those who are suffering, you may ask yourself, "What can I do to help?"

Ours is an action culture. The emphasis is on *doing*. And when a problem occurs, the emphasis is on *solving* the problem as quickly as possible. Very often, however, there is little or nothing that can be done to quickly resolve the painful and complex problems people experience: you cannot bring a husband back to life; you cannot make love grow in a marriage where it has died; you cannot make terminal illness go away. As a result, you may feel completely at a loss to do anything that greatly helps a person who is engulfed in such a crisis. Like most of us, you may say, "Let me know if there's anything I can do." Then, as you walk away, you may feel upset or guilty that a person who obviously hurts has refused your offer of help.

You may respond in many ways you are not aware of when others are hurting: you may stay away; you may try to cheer them up or keep them busy; you may avoid talking about the problem. Beneath much of your behavior may be fear of the pain that person is experiencing or feelings of inadequacy and guilt because you cannot solve the problem.

The first false assumption that must be put to rest if you want to help someone who hurts is that you can help only by somehow solving the painful problem that person is experiencing. Our culture has become accustomed, from television and the movies, to quick-fix solutions for even the most difficult and complex problems. Your frustration may increase rapidly when such problems cannot be resolved as promptly and successfully as they are on TV!

Seward Hiltner makes an important distinction between a *healing* role and a *sustaining* role in ministering to a person who hurts.[1] This distinction is important because very often your role may be that of sustainer, which is not as gratifying as healer. Even when a person does find healing for the hurt and overcomes the crisis, the healing process is often painfully slow and difficult, with many setbacks along the way. It requires patience and endurance on your part to offer the consistent quality in a relationship that will enable a person to work through a painful loss or disability.

The fact is, though, you are not obligated to solve the crisis that overwhelms another person. You can best help by being there in supportive ways that help mobilize that person's own resources and faith to cope with the crisis. You can learn to develop the personal skills that encourage a person involved in a crisis to work through and overcome the crisis himself or herself. The skills needed to help are the subject of the rest of this book.

Any person who hurts over a major loss, illness, or injury needs to hear four key messages from someone:

- "You are not alone."
- "Your feelings matter."
- "All is not lost."
- "You can still help yourself."

In order to effectively convey these crucial messages, several essential skills will be identified and discussed. These helping skills will be very briefly defined here, and more complete discussion and examples will be provided in the succeeding chapters.

HELPING SKILLS[2]

1. Inviting—Encouraging the person to express a need or problem.
2. Acknowledging—Commenting to let the person know you are listening ("yes," "uh huh").
3. Offering Assistance—Letting another person know that you want to help and you are willing to help.
4. Attending (Attentive listening)—Letting another know by your behavior that you are giving complete attention to what they are expressing, both verbally and nonverbally.
5. Reflecting—Giving another person a "playback" of the feelings and the content you hear him or her expressing.
6. Exploring, probing—Using questions or leading statements to develop more information about the feelings or problem of another.
7. Testing—Stating what you think you understand another to be saying so the other person can clarify or confirm your perceptions.
8. Identifying—Letting the other person know that you have had some experience or feeling similar to that being expressed.
9. Discussing the helping relationship—Stating and examining problems or feelings arising from your relationship with the other person.
10. Confronting—Presenting the other person with possible blind spots, self-defeating behavior or inconsistencies that need to be faced.

11. Stating the problem—Sharing with the other person your perception of the problem, with a brief summary statement.

12. Identifying resources—Describing various sources of help and insight related to the problem the person has expressed.

13. Planning for action—Exploring and defining with the person a step-by-step process aimed at overcoming or coping with the problem defined.

14. Reinforcing and affirming—Identifying the gains, insights, and positive efforts put forth in seeking the solution to a problem; giving personal affirmation.

These helping skills are actions that can be learned by anyone committed to learning them. A significant level of self-awareness and discipline is required to develop them. Usually the help of others is needed to learn the impact your actions have on other people; therefore, it is important that you seek out some training experience with others also committed to developing these skills. Through discipline and growth we learn how to make love active in our relationships. The church is the best place to develop these skills of caring love.[3]

A HELPING RELATIONSHIP

For our purposes in this book, a helping relationship will be defined as a relationship in which there is sufficient trust and understanding to allow a person or persons with specific problems to receive strength, insight, and resources to cope with a problem and overcome its destructive effects. From a Christian perspective, we will assume that a helping relationship will be characterized by the following:

1. A focus on change. People are capable of making change, for the better or for the worse. This includes changes in behavior, attitude, location, relationships, values, and

beliefs. Responsibility for making change in any of these areas rests with the person involved, however limited the options might be.

2. Emphasis on the future. While the wounds of the past require attention, the potential for growth and healing lies in the future. Without a clear vision of the possibilities the future holds, there is little motivation for constructive change in the present. Consequently, hopes and dreams are an important focus for the helping process.

3. A deep respect for people. Every person has God-given worth and deserves respect. Therefore, the feelings, attitudes, needs, and values of another person deserve to be taken seriously regardless of how different from your own they might be.

4. Faith in God as a vital source of renewal and strength. There is a God who always cares. This deep belief in God who made himself known in Jesus of Nazareth is one of the most important resources in a helping relationship. God as "a very present help in trouble" is a most reassuring element in the Christian faith.

On the basis of these assumptions, we will discuss the helping process. While the emphasis will be placed on your behavior as a helper, it should be noted that the genuineness with which you relate to one who hurts is a very important ingredient. Listening skills can help you develop a deeper understanding of what a person is thinking and feeling, but those skills are of little real help unless you possess an honest desire to respect and understand that person. Likewise, your attempts to convey acceptance will fail miserably if your real agenda is to manipulate a person to think, feel, or behave in a manner you can accept. Your own openness, honesty, and personal warmth are key elements in the challenging task of helping anyone who is hurting.

Rather than presenting a detailed clinical approach to helping relationships, this book will discuss the powerful importance of friendship. Everyone needs friends. And the qualities
that make friendship strong—affection, respect, trust, consis-
tency, warmth, honesty, empathy—are also the qualities that
offer healing and hope to a person who hurts. If you want to
help that person, then learn first how to be a friend. It usually
takes a long time for a person to overcome a major crisis or
loss. Only the enduring commitment of friendship is strong
enough to provide the patience and persistence required to be
there and listen during times of discouragement, pain, and
loneliness.

NOTES

1. Seward Hiltner, *Preface to Pastoral Theology* (Nashville: Abingdon Press, 1958), chaps. 6 and 7. In this landmark work, Dr. Hiltner
presents three important aspects of the task of pastoral support of
those in need: healing, sustaining, and guiding. He gives very useful
insights into the particular circumstances in which each of these styles
is most beneficial.

2. Dennis Kinlaw, *Helping Skills for Human Resource Development*
(San Diego: University Associates, Inc., 1981). These categories for
helping skills are used in the training manual developed by Dennis
Kinlaw. This training manual provides a detailed training process, using written material, exercises, and audio tapes. The training process
presented in the manual is an especially clear and practical approach
to training which can be implemented with lay persons in the church
or in other settings.

3. A thorough and well-organized training process designed for use
in the local church has been developed by Stephen Ministries, Inc.
The Stephen Series provides a training process and a system for
implementing helping relationships as they are described in this book.
More information about this excellent training process may be ob-
tained by contacting Stephen Ministries, 1325 Boland, St. Louis, MO
63117.

1

LONELINESS AND ISOLATION

"You are not alone"

Marjorie had been alone for more than a year since her husband Arthur had died following a stroke. All of her friends at church thought she had adjusted adequately to the loss. Her son, who lived several hundred miles away, was assured frequently that she was managing very well on her own. She had moved into an apartment and had become active in a number of volunteer groups.

One Sunday after church, one of Marjorie's friends asked her how she was doing. Marjorie answered, "Do you really want to know?" Her friend answered, "Of course!" So Marjorie proceeded to tell her how difficult the past several months had been.

"I should be doing fine, I know," she said, "but I just feel so desperately alone all the time! I don't sleep well at night, so I'm tired all day. I don't have much of an appetite. . . . Even when I'm around other people I still feel all alone . . . since Arthur died." She then went on to tell how she felt all the more lonely when she was around other couples and families.

Loneliness, or a feeling of isolation, is a very common experience for someone who suffers a painful loss or serious illness. This sense of loneliness is itself the source of much emotional pain, often with accompanying feelings of uselessness, rejection, and depression. Although we usually associate loneliness with old age, there are many other times when the feeling of being alone is a serious problem:

- When marital separation and divorce occur
- When the last child leaves home for college or marriage
- When death intrudes to take away a spouse, close friend, parent, or child
- When serious illness or injury results in disability
- When a career choice or opportunity is lost

In any of these situations, one is likely to feel isolated by the anxiety and pain of his or her predicament. The challenge for you as a person who cares is to penetrate the walls that isolate without intruding where you are not wanted.

Can you remember the last time you hit your thumbnail with a hammer (accidentally, I hope)? Have you ever had an intense headache or toothache or severe abdominal pain? If so, you can recall that, momentarily at least, your distress demanded your full attention. Everything and everyone around you were shut out of your awareness by your pain, and your concentration was on easing your pain. Those who experience the emotional pain brought on by physical illness, personal loss, or disability are similarly consumed by the emotional pain *they* feel. They build thick walls that tend to shut others out until their isolation adds the pain of loneliness to their original hurt.

COMMON RESPONSES

Your purpose when friends or loved ones are hurting and alone will usually be to provide some assurance that you are truly with them. But that is easier said than done. The walls of pain, fear, and resentment that isolate them may be all but impenetrable.

When you offer to help a friend or family member, it is painful and baffling to be told to mind your own business. Very often when your help is refused you will feel angry and rejected. Your reaction may be to withdraw or to attack, either one of which serves only to confirm the isolation of the person you want to help.

An offer of help to a recently widowed man may be met with stony silence, a terse "I'm fine," or even a reply such as, "I'll have to handle it myself." A natural reaction on your part to any of these may be to withdraw from him completely with a polite, "Call me if I can help."

If you are going to be of any help to this person, it is important to recognize that many mixed feelings just under the surface make it very difficult for him to openly accept an offer of help. The loss he has experienced may have left him wondering if it is really worth it to be close to another person. He may be feeling angry about the unfairness of life in dealing him such a loss. He may have been taught that a real man shouldn't need any sympathy or support. Or he may simply be feeling so hurt and empty that he doesn't believe anyone can be of any help.

Whatever his feelings, it is clear that he will not easily allow anyone to come close enough to help ease his loneliness and isolation. Nor is it easy for you to respond in a helpful fashion to the withdrawal or open hostility displayed by the one in need of support. Whatever the situation, there are several forms of response at this point that are almost certainly *not* helpful:

1. "Oh, cheer up!" (Or, "It can't be *that* bad!")—This response can take many forms: humor, teasing, or coaxing. But its aim is usually to make the person feel better. Sometimes it will momentarily help lonely people, but it fails to take seriously their deep concerns or needs and will often stop further personal discussion. Lonely people may prefer to play along with you rather than be left alone, so your need to cheer someone up will be met while their deep needs go untouched.

2. "Let's talk about more pleasant things!"—There seems to

be a deep-seated belief that people who are hurting and lonely need to be distracted from their troubles. If these people are kept busy, they won't have time to dwell on their loneliness or feel sorry for themselves, so they will feel better. We feel also that if we avoid talking about their distress, we help avoid depressing them! Both of these are serious misconceptions that prompt us to relate to people in pain in a way that may drive them deeper into their loneliness and isolation. Their original painful loss or disability is never resolved, only covered over by much activity.

A common example of this tendency is the "conspiracy of silence" that often follows the death of a spouse or other family member. Very often a recent widow or widower will express anguish over the fact that her or his friends avoid any mention of the deceased loved one. "It's as though he never existed!" said one widow. "Can't people see that I want to talk about him? . . . I need to talk about him. I haven't forgotten him! Even when I mention his name my friends get nervous and turn the conversation to something else."

This kind of "helping" behavior often cuts people off from those whose support they need, leaving them alone to work through feelings of loss and grief. Its net effect is to say, "If you want to be with me you have to give up your hurt." This way the helper does not have to get involved with the deep feelings of the other person.

3. "What you should do is . . ."—There are many ways advice may be given to a person who is hurting and isolated. The problem is that most advice fails to respond to the deep and basic loneliness the person is feeling. The advice or suggestion may secretly say to that person, "You should feel different by now," or "I don't understand why you don't try to help yourself." These messages serve only to deepen the loneliness the person feels. Until we are able to communicate respect for and

understanding of the person's feelings, our advice is likely to fall on deaf ears and reinforce the walls of isolation.

4. "Let me know if there's anything I can do . . ."—This message, too, comes in many forms. It is usually a genuine expression of concern and availability to help. The problem is that it leaves the initiative with those who are hurting at a time when they are least able to ask for help. Pain and isolation have an immobilizing effect on a person. It is not unusual to hear from one who has been through a time of deep suffering, "If you think your friend *might* need help, take the initiative. Go to him. That means more than anyone could ever possibly imagine!"

We need to realize how difficult it is for most people to ask for help, even under normal conditions. In a time of crisis, it requires a monumental effort to ask for help when people feel that no one could possibly understand their confused and complex feelings. Asking for any specific form of assistance often becomes a last resort due to a fear of rejection. Thus, even the invitation to call for help can be another burden that confirms the isolated position of the one who suffers the effects of a painful loss or serious illness.

HELPFUL RESPONSES

There *are* positive actions we can take that will effectively convey a more helpful message to the person who feels hurt and alone. It is important to keep in mind that it does *not* require a lot of sophistication or eloquence to convey these messages—only a grasp of simple, basic ways of communicating that are likely to get through to the person who is isolated and hurting.

Inviting and Acknowledging. It is important that you make yourself available as a listening friend for a person who feels

alone. You may begin by reporting to the person the signs of
distress you have detected ("You seem to have a lot on your
mind today") in order to invite response. Or you may make a
more direct invitation: "I know you are going through some
tough times, and if you want to talk with someone I'm willing
to listen." Or even an expression of your desire to be of help
can open the way: "I surely do want to help if I can."

If the person who hurts expresses some of the pain felt, it is
then very important to let him or her know you have heard,
even if you don't know what else to say. Any response, a nod or
a brief reply, can help the person know that you are listening
and that you are willing to hear more.

Attending. The most basic way of reaching out to lonely people
is simply to pay attention to what they are saying—verbally
and nonverbally. It sounds simple, but noticing both spoken
and unspoken clues to what a person is feeling requires practice and concentration. It's much easier to assume you understand and go on from there without checking your assumptions.
Even for the most perceptive helper, the skills for attending are
not easy to acquire.

It is important to listen carefully to the hidden message a
person expresses as well as to the surface content of what he or
she says. That means noticing the tone of voice, gestures, facial
expression, and body posture as well as the words. It's true
that words are used to conceal as well as to reveal. Often a person who is isolated and hurting will use words to mask the
pain. But a friend who pays careful attention can hear the
underlying feeling in the tone of voice or notice a dull or
faraway look in the eyes, a detached attitude, or a score of other
clues to the inner world of the person.

In paying attention to the person you want to help, the focus
should be on the "here and now." You may be distracted by

what happened yesterday or might happen tomorrow (both of which are important), but they take you away from what this person is feeling right now. In fact, a conscientious helper may become so involved in trying to resolve yesterday's hurts or plan for tomorrow that he or she may miss today's loneliness.

It is most important that you show the hurting person that you are paying attention. The aim is to be fully present with the person in such a way that he or she is aware of your focused attention. Although you cannot control the perceptions of other people, you can express your presence with and availability to others in such a way that they will experience your full concentration.

Physical posture is an important way to demonstrate availability to a person. Your level of involvement with another person is conveyed by eye contact, relaxed posture, gestures, facial expression, and facing the person straight on. In fact, these may do more to say "I am with you" than any words you can say.

Touching. The most direct way to express presence and availability is by touching. Physical touch is a much more direct way than words of saying "I am with you." Especially to a person who is in pain and feeling desolate, a gentle touch on the shoulder or hand can show caring and concern. A caring touch can often penetrate the walls that isolate a person when nothing else can. This very crucial form of communication may be seen in the hospital where the husband or wife of a person who is critically ill simply stays with the patient holding her hand or stroking his forehead. With or without words, powerful and helpful messages are shared in this way.

Care must be taken, however, to respect the need for distance any person may have. It takes careful and sensitive attention to discover the level of contact a person can safely allow.

Probing personal questions or physical touch may threaten a person who has not had time to develop trust in your intentions or sensitivity. If there is any doubt, it is appropriate to ask such questions as, "Where would you like me to sit?" or "Would you rather not talk about it right now?" Such questions help to communicate respect for the needs of the person you want to help. Until people feel that respect from you, they will be unlikely to accept your efforts to help.

Reflecting. Besides paying attention and demonstrating your attentiveness, reflecting feelings may be the most helpful way of letting people know you are there. If you can state clearly and accurately the feelings people are expressing—verbally or nonverbally—you will make it clear that you are paying attention, and also that you are accurately perceiving at least a part of what they are experiencing. When people express their pain, with or without words, it is important for them to know you are hearing what they say.

Reflecting involves stating as simply as possible what you perceive the person to be feeling. It may be done with just a word or a phrase: ". . . Pretty low today, huh?" or "You're feeling pretty much alone." A reflecting response requires no explanation or elaboration, for it is offered simply to give the other a clue that says "I hear you."

A reflecting response may give people the freedom and reassurance they need to be increasingly open with their feelings. Yet it does not force them to divulge more of their inner world than they are ready to share. In fact, you may reflect the nonverbal messages a person is giving and let him or her know immediately that you are interested in joining: "You seem to be preoccupied with something today." Again, take care to avoid intruding upon someone's privacy. An initiative that says "I am available" is inviting but not pushy. Unless you know the person rather well, it will take some time to develop the comfort level necessary for him or her to be open with personal feelings.

Avoiding stylized or trite reflecting statements may be important as well. People who are hurting and lonely may withdraw when a "technique" is used on them. Statements that begin with "You feel . . ." or "I hear you saying . . ." are likely to sound like gimmicks to most people. But if you can't think of any other way to reflect feelings, go ahead and use them!

Identifying. One additional way to join the person who feels isolated is through identification or self-disclosure. Self-disclosure means selectively sharing with another your own feelings, thoughts, or experiences that relate directly to what the other person is feeling. Obviously, it is important to be sure you accurately perceive what he or she is feeling; otherwise, the experience you share may simply confirm that you don't really understand those feelings. You should take precautions to avoid shifting the focus of conversation to *your* experience.

Many people will inquire about you simply to shift the focus away from themselves for a few moments. This may provide a relaxed give-and-take tone to the conversation that momentarily takes the focus off of their pain. While this can be a very healthy development in the conversation, it may be important for you to make it clear that you are not trying to avoid the painful feelings the other has expressed.

For example, if you say, "I felt that kind of emptiness when my youngest son went away to college," a widow you are talking with may ask about that experience. It is appropriate to share something about your own experience but eventually you must shift back to her fresh sense of loss.

It can be very reassuring for a widow who is depressed or

anxious and feeling isolated to hear that someone else has been
through a similar experience. A common reaction upon hearing that her feelings and experiences are not unusual is "You
mean I'm not the only one who has ever felt like this?" She
may feel a great sense of relief in knowing that her experience is
shared by others.

"God cares for you." One of the most important and lasting
messages a lonely and hurting person may need to hear is
"God is with you." Yet it may be one of the most difficult
messages for anyone in pain to hear. Common questions you
may hear from one who is hurting are "Why did God let this
happen to me?" or "What kind of God could let this happen to
me?"

You might be tempted at that point to rush to God's defense,
explaining that God is not to blame for the pain and loneliness
your friend is going through. But these attempts at persuasion
are likely to be unconvincing at best. It is probably best to
acknowledge the anguish in the question and confess your own
inability to understand why. Psalms 22 and 46 are cries of
anguish that may be very helpful reminders that others have
been in the same position. More important, they make it clear
that it is all right to release these feelings of anguish, and even
anger, to God.

Reassuring someone about God's presence and care should
never be a substitute for your presence and availability to a
person who is alone and hurting. Saying "I'll be praying for
you" is too often a way of keeping a person at a safe distance
when we feel at a loss to do anything helpful. The Christian
faith is centered on the fact that God's grace and love are expressed in human relationships: "The Word became flesh and
dwelt among us . . ." (John 1:14), and the presence and availability of God's love is still mediated, however imperfectly, by

those who respond to this love and accept the responsibility to carry that same love to others who need it.

The implication is this: the presence and love of God can be most effectively communicated to a lonely and troubled person when that person has already experienced your presence and availability. The attention and respect you show as a listener give credibility to your words of assurance that God is available; they give you the right to be heard when your friend who is hurting is ready to listen.

Though it may sound simple to give complete attention to a person who is hurting, it is not easy. It requires energy and discipline to focus your attention on the pain that a person is experiencing and to show respect for his or her feelings. Many who want to help are quick to refute any "negative" feelings such as fear, anger, anxiety, or depression: "You shouldn't feel that way!" If you want to help, the first step is to be fully present with the one who is hurting. Through your attentiveness, touch, and physical presence, you can convey the message, "You are not alone." That message then forms the basis for other helping messages.

2

UNWELCOME EMOTIONS

"Your feelings matter"

Ralph and Sarah had been married thirty-seven years when Sarah discovered a lump in her breast. After an examination, her doctor scheduled her for a biopsy which revealed a malignant tumor. Within a few days Sarah underwent radical breast surgery.

There followed many anxious months for Ralph and Sarah as she received treatments to prevent the spread of cancer cells. But in spite of the treatments, within a year new evidence of cancer was found in her lungs and liver. Sarah underwent a new series of treatments, but the results were not very encouraging. She and Ralph realized that their worst fear might come true: Sarah might be terminally ill.

During the ordeal of chemotherapy and its many days of weakness and sickness, most of Ralph and Sarah's friends admired their stiff-upper-lip attitude about their situation. Neither Sarah nor Ralph expressed any complaint or disappointment about her illness, and they tried to maintain a routine as nearly normal as possible. The conversations between Ralph and Sarah emphasized the positive and did not include the underlying fears and anger each felt at times. Ralph stayed with Sarah even when she had to be hospitalized due to weakness and medical complications.

When Sarah finally died, Ralph reacted with resignation. Physically and emotionally exhausted from the many months of caring for Sarah during the terminal stage of her illness, he told the minister that he didn't want a long funeral service with a lot of emotional music. He did not shed any tears in the presence of friends or family members. "Those things are to be done in private," he said.

For several weeks after Sarah's funeral, Ralph seemed stable but a little detached. When friends expressed sympathy, he responded by saying something like, "Sarah wouldn't want me to spend a lot of time crying about this." Most friends would respond in silent agreement and move away from Ralph.

About a month after Sarah's funeral, the pastor stopped by Ralph's home to visit. After a few minutes of pleasant conversation, the pastor mentioned Sarah and stated that Ralph must be "pretty lonely." Ralph stiffened and looked angry for a moment; tears welled up in his eyes. Then he burst out, "I just don't understand why this happened to her! . . . She was a good woman. She didn't deserve . . ." He sobbed and buried his face in his hands.

Within a few minutes Ralph apologized to his pastor for the emotional outburst. He followed his apology with several statements he thought the pastor might respond to, such as, "I'm sure God knows best." But the pastor focused on the deep feelings Ralph had expressed that acknowledged the hurt and loneliness he felt over Sarah's death. Then he offered to visit with Ralph on a weekly basis to help him sort through some of those feelings and questions that were on his mind.

It took several visits with the pastor before Ralph could express his feelings very freely or without apology. But as he did he found that he regained some interests in life that he had not thought about for months. After a few months, he was able to talk with friends about Sarah and how much he missed her, though he would still retreat when he became choked up with emotion.

Ralph looks back now to those visits with his pastor as a

turning point for him: "Until then I thought it wasn't very grown-up to show my feelings. But I didn't realize how my emotions built up on me and weighed me down. I only wish that Sarah and I had been able to have a good cry together while she was still alive. We missed something important because we kept what we were feeling from each other."

HIDING NEGATIVE FEELINGS

As children we learn that expressing the strong emotions of fear, anger, and even sadness can often get us in a lot of trouble. Depending upon how they are expressed, these emotions can bring disapproval or rejection from the adults upon whom we depend. The task of stifling or suppressing our emotions becomes necessary in order for us to be accepted by those in authority.

The two most common ways of stifling emotions are *denying* and *discounting*. Both of these methods minimize or neutralize the effect emotions have on the lives of those who see feelings as negative. It should be noted that each method requires the cooperation of others to some extent in order to keep it going. Whenever someone is denying or discounting feelings, there will usually be other people around who encourage that behavior. It is important to understand not only the fears people have of their own emotions but also the risks they may face with their friends if they change the way they express their emotions. Both denying and discounting work for the comfort of others and have rewards that go along with them.

It isn't quite that simple though. Emotions are too much a God-given part of our make-up to be completely discarded, even with much effort. Especially when unexpected changes and crises occur, strong emotional responses are touched off. These powerful feelings can upset the equilibrium of our lives completely unless we are able to recognize, accept, and express them in some constructive manner. To deal constructively with emotions we need to take them seriously as important parts of our personal make-up.

It is precisely those "negative feelings"—anger, fear, and sadness—that engulf a person who is suffering a tragic loss, physical illness, injury, or any big disappointment in life. The feelings of outrage, sadness, and fear following the death of a spouse can overpower a person who has successfully choked off those feelings in other situations. In fact, one commonly expressed fear during the time of mourning by such a person is of losing control over emotions. Very often that fear is accompanied by a sense of shame. In the midst of grief, a bereaved spouse can often be heard to say, "I'm sorry! I'm just being such a baby" or "Don't mind me. I'll get hold of myself." This feeling of embarrassment is often much stronger in men, who feel it is not very manly to cry.

How should you go about helping a person who is experiencing these intense and uncontrollable feelings? How can you give encouragement to someone who seems to be at the mercy of his or her feelings? Should you just stay away for a while until those feelings are under control? (This happens a lot.) Or should you try to keep the person busy or distracted and not even acknowledge the presence of sadness or anger? (This happens a lot, too.)

Much will depend upon how you, the helper, feel about these strong emotions. If you would rather avoid any expression of anger, fear, or sadness—especially if there is no way to quickly resolve the feelings—then you may not be able to help that person cope with the waves of deep and powerful emotion. If you do not take these feelings seriously as you offer your help, you may very well encourage the denial and discounting of feelings which the person does already. The result could be to slow the healing process. But when you are able to communicate interest in and respect for the feelings of the person you wish to assist, you may help open the way for new healing and growth to take place.

Denial. Denial refers to attempts to convince oneself and others that unpleasant feelings do not exist. Such negative feelings as anger, fear, and sadness have no place in the experience of a person who engages in denial. Children who are rejected—pushed away or hushed—by their parents whenever they show anger, children who are ridiculed or shamed when they show fear, are learning that these feelings are not an acceptable part of human experience. These children often develop a remarkable capacity to push such feelings out of their conscious lives most of the time. To maintain self-respect and the approval of others the offending emotions are given no validity. By using denial people tell themselves, "I do not (or will not) *feel* that emotion."

One of the most common forms of denial is overcontrol. A typical example of overcontrol is when people become very calm in a frustrating or frightening situation. You can almost hear them saying, "I will not be afraid!" or "I am not angry!" These people are often lavishly rewarded for being "cool under fire" or even-tempered, and there may be many ways their high level of control benefits them in handling everyday annoyances and emergencies. They are seldom at the mercy of their feelings. What begins, however, as an attempt to cope constructively with strong emotions can gradually develop into an exaggerated and unhelpful form of denial. Instead of saying, "I will not be controlled by my emotions," they become more negative and say "I will not experience these emotions." When their self-control becomes so rigid that these people can no longer feel the unwanted emotional response to a stressful situation, they have developed a blind spot in their lives. Now they can remain totally unaware of their own anger, fear, or sadness due to the heavy controls they place on these feelings.

Another form denial takes is the super-reasonable approach to any emotionally charged situation. The basic assumption of super-reasonable people is that if something is not logical, it isn't real. If these people cannot explain their feelings, then those feelings have no validity. The first step in this approach is to express no feeling that cannot be justified logically. The second step is to feel no feeling that cannot be justified. It is as though they use an anesthetic to numb feelings that are not reasonable. It is so important to be reasonable in our culture that many people see emotions as untrustworthy because they are not rational. The super-reasonable approach is an attempt to banish upsetting emotions that threaten one's apparent strength or respectability.

Each of these styles of denial may prove valuable to a person in coping with upsetting situations. Adults tend to approve of and reward children who show no anger or fear, and those rewards encourage further control over emotions. The conflicts of the teenage years are confusing and unsettling; denying strong emotions, such as hatred or love, can help to keep a young person out of trouble. There is always a demand for adults who "don't make waves" by expressing contrary feelings too openly or emphatically. Consider the number of movie or television heroes who are "cool," detached, unemotional characters—sometimes even when they are making love! There are many rewards in our culture for those who succeed in stifling and denying feelings. But exaggerated control leads to a denial that the feelings even exist. The inevitable result is an accumulation of unclaimed, unacknowledged feelings that are stored rather than given appropriate expression.

Since emotions do not go away simply because we ignore them, the real trouble arises when there is a crisis in the life of the person who denies feelings. When a physical breakdown or a tragic loss such as the death of a spouse occurs, this person is often flooded with powerful emotions that can no longer be denied. These deep feelings are often confusing and frightening because they cannot be controlled or stifled. These people may feel as though they are losing control of their whole lives when they are overpowered by their own feelings of sorrow, fear, or anger. In fact, it is not unusual for a man or woman in crisis to expend a great deal of emotional energy trying to control the unacceptable feelings. A feeling of exhaustion and helplessness is often the result of this type of struggle.

For people in crisis, these strong emotions are often compounded by the fear of being deserted by others. At this time more than any other, they need the support of close friends and family members. Yet they commonly express the fear that people won't want to be around them if they are too emotional. So we have the irony of people who are deeply hurt, hiding the feelings they think will scare away those on whom they rely for strength and friendship. The truth is that experience too often justifies the fear that friends will avoid a person if he or she expresses too much emotion.

We should recognize that there are many statements we make in trying to offer comfort and support that can reinforce denial in people who are hurting. Clichés like "This too will pass" and "Don't worry. God has everything under control" may only push them to try still harder to get rid of the feelings of sorrow and fear they are already fighting. And we may indicate by such statements that they are right to suppress those feelings as inappropriate and unacceptable. Words we offer to provide assurance of God's presence and care may even instill a sense of guilt in others if they dare feel any fear, sorrow, or anger.

On the other hand, we need to recognize that a person who has lived by denying feelings for many years cannot easily give up that pattern. It is unfair to expect a person who has learned to handle most situations in life without acknowledging strong emotions to suddenly learn to express those feelings at a time of crisis. If we want to help such people, we should also be aware that putting pressure on them to "let it all out" may only deepen the crisis they are experiencing. The crisis situation may offer an opportunity to change the pattern of denial, but that change will not usually happen overnight. Keep in mind that these people may not even admit their feelings, and only over time can they come to accept the importance and power of their unclaimed emotions.

There are several things you can do that will help people who deny their feelings to recognize and accept their own emotions. But let's look first at the closely related pattern of discounting and see how that pattern may differ from the denial pattern. Then we will consider helpful responses to both patterns.

Discounting. Discounting feelings is similar in many ways to denying feelings. The difference is that people who discount are not only aware of the feelings but also will usually admit that they are present. They understate their feelings rather than deny them and regard emotion as an unimportant part of experience. They may be so committed to the value of reason over emotion that the only way they can express emotion is if they can explain it rationally. They may also believe that certain emotions, such as anger, fear, sadness, and even romantic feelings, are unacceptable to God. So they see these feelings as a nuisance, a necessary evil, detrimental to one's relationship with God.

People who discount their own feelings will tend to respond, "It doesn't matter," when asked how they feel. They will seldom voice their feelings in a conversation, and when they do, will often apologize for them. Likewise, they may feel very

guilty whenever they state any strong feelings. They have
given up the right to express any strong emotions, though they
are at least vaguely aware of having those feelings.

Not only will these people discount their own feelings, they
will frequently devalue the emotions of others as well. You
may hear them say, "Why do you feel that way?" or "You
shouldn't feel like that!" when someone expresses emotions
that trouble them. Their underlying assumption seems to be
that certain emotions are not entitled to expression. Any sign
of anger may denote to them a threat of violent conflict or rejection; sorrow may pose the threat of overwhelming and immobilizing depression; and fear may represent the presence of
cowardly weakness. So these feelings are given no place to take
root in the experience of people who discount them. They may
even state their belief that weak people are controlled by feelings while strong people are controlled by reason.

The net effect of discounting feelings may be very similar to
that of denying feelings: confusion and fear when a crisis sets
off waves of uncontrollable emotion. People who believe it is
weak to have certain strong emotions may be afraid of being
seen as weak or unstable by others. Much energy may be spent
apologizing for any evidence of the feelings they consider to be
offensive. Many times when they are hurting, people who discount emotions will also be unable to pray. The presence of
unacceptable emotions cuts them off from God because they
feel that God will not hear them when such feelings are present. As noted in chapter one, this sense of isolation and alienation from God can deepen the crisis for such people.

HELPFUL RESPONSES

To help people who discount their feelings, you need to
recognize how important it is to them to avoid being seen as
weak. It takes time and patience to establish the level of trust
that will allow them to expose the hurt, grief, or fear they feel

without being overcome by shame and guilt. Once that trust is present, there are several ways you can convey the message "Your feelings matter." By recognizing and respecting the feelings they struggle with, you can join them and help them cope with the pain they are living through.

Attending. Before you can respond to feelings, you must notice and recognize them. All of the verbal and nonverbal behavior of the person who is hurting should be observed as potentially revealing of inner feelings. A subdued or somber tone of voice, downcast eyes, clenched fists, and tight facial expression may reveal inner feelings of sadness, anger, shame, anxiety, or fear of losing control. As you talk with the person you want to help, you should make note of any behavior that may denote the presence of strong hidden feelings. This information should not be used to make a final "diagnosis," but as clues to what *may* be going on inside that person. Jumping to conclusions about what someone is feeling at this point can greatly hinder the development of an open relationship.

Reflecting what you observe can be a very helpful way of acknowledging the feelings of other people and showing your respect for their inner emotions. Reflecting involves telling another person, concisely, your perception of the feelings you are hearing. Examples of reflecting statements are:

- "You seem to be pretty concerned about what is expected of you."
- "It sounds like the doctor's news was pretty devastating to you."
- "It seems you're pretty upset about this whole situation."
- "I hear a lot of sadness in your voice when you talk about your son."

One thing you should avoid as you reflect is the kind of statement that sounds like a gimmick. Statements beginning with "I hear you saying . . ." or "You're feeling . . ." may be a good way to practice focusing on the feelings of another person, but may sound stilted when someone is struggling with deep feelings. Make sure your tone of voice is compatible with the message you want to convey. A matter-of-fact tone of voice at this point can discourage rather than encourage the expression of deep feeling. Reflecting statements should also be offered tentatively at first to avoid the impression that you are trying to diagnose or label the person. The purpose of reflecting is to let the person know that you are listening and that what he or she is feeling matters to you; it invites the person to share further feelings if he or she wishes.

Probing is another way of inviting people to express what they are feeling. A probing response further explores what people are feeling and invites (not forces) further sharing of feelings. As people who are hurting begin to express feelings about their problems, a probing response can continue the process. It is important to emphasize that the probing or searching you do as a helper should *follow* rather than lead the person you want to help. Early in a conversation about a problem, probing questions can often divert the conversation to your agenda rather than your friend's. The more open-ended your probing statements and questions, the more likely you will be to receive honest expressions of feeling in return. Probing can be either open or closed.

Examples of open and closed probes:

Closed Question:
   "How old were you when your mother died?"

Open-ended Question:
   "What effect did your mother's death have on you?"

Open-ended Request:
   "Tell me more about the events that have had an impact on your life recently."

Closed Question:

"Have you ever tried praying when you feel depressed?"

Open-ended Question:

"What do you usually do when you begin feeling depressed?"

Open-ended Request:

"I'm interested in how this feeling of sadness comes over you."

A closed question limits the response you receive. It may require only a yes or no answer or very specific information. The closed probe can be more helpful later in the helping process to focus on specific information or solutions. The open-ended probe is usually much more helpful as a means of inviting the person you want to help to talk about his or her problem. It requires practice and discipline to develop an open-ended approach, however, and a training group can be most helpful in developing this skill.[1]

A healthy combination of reflecting and probing responses is an excellent way to explore the feelings of people who are hurting. As feelings are expressed in conversation, reflecting what you hear can be a way of reassuring friends that you are staying with them. Probing responses assure them that you want to both hear more and better understand what they are experiencing.

Testing or checking-out your perceptions is an important step in developing an understanding of the feelings of the other person. Testing simply means confirming your perception by asking direct questions that may be open or closed.

Communicating respect for the feelings expressed plays a vitally important role in the helping relationship. For most of us the recognition and acknowledgment of feelings without evaluation or rebuttal does not come easily. But, especially in the early stages of a helping relationship, it is important to avoid showing disrespect for the feelings the person expresses. The following are examples of some commonly used ways of showing *disrespect* for feelings that are shared:

1. "Why do you feel that way?" (Demands an explanation)
2. "Oh, surely there is something good happening right now, too!" (Discounting)
3. "Maybe things aren't as bad as they seem right now." (Denial)

In each example the message is given that the feelings expressed need to be defended. Unless there is a very high level of trust, the helping process will often end here with the other person feeling either wrong or misunderstood.

Withholding evaluation or rebuttal is the first step in communicating respect. Responses that show respect reflect and probe, but nonverbal behavior that demonstrates attentiveness and interest in what the person says is also important. Eye contact and a posture of comfortable attention encourage the other person to share the hurt with you.

FEELINGS CAN BE
CHANGED

The glorious truth about the human make-up is that feelings can be changed. Even the most powerful and destructive emotions can, in time, be stripped of their destructive power. But emotions that are held tightly under control cannot be transformed into a healthy source of growth and strength. Painful and powerful emotions must be exposed and claimed before the healing process can begin. As Henri Nouwen has pointed out: "Only those who face their wounded condition can be available for healing and so enter a new way of living."[2]

Consider the progression expressed in Psalm 22, A Psalm of David:

"My God, my God, why have you forsaken me?
　Why are you so far from saving me,
　so far from the words of my groaning?
O my God, I cry out by day but you do not answer,
　by night, and am not silent."

(v. 1)

This cry of isolation and pain expresses the desolation many
people feel when they are immersed in tragic circumstances.
David's cry could have been cut short by friends who pointed
out that God had, in fact, not forsaken him at all. But those
feelings needed to be given full expression in order for the
work of inner restoration to begin. Then the expression of
loneliness and bitterness gives way to the recognition that God
is with him, and cares for him—even as he gives expression to
his suffering:

"For He has not despised or disdained
　the suffering of the afflicted one;
he has not hidden his face from him,
　but has listened to his cry for help."

(v. 24)

Unexpressed pain and resentment from past experiences are
often crippling sources of emotional blockage in many people.
The healing they need can begin as they are given the acceptance and encouragement to expose their painful feelings.
When these deep hurts are brought out into the open, they
become available for the grace of God to heal and transform.
That grace can be concretely expressed by your presence,
availability, and acceptance of your friends in the midst of
their pain.

The natural tendency on the part of the helper is to correct
or refute the strong emotions expressed by persons who are
hurting. But it is important at first to encourage the expression
of feeling without evaluation or rebuttal. It requires discipline

to listen to distorted or exaggerated reactions and to respond with understanding rather than rebuttal. There is certainly a time to confront and challenge distortions and overreactions, but intervening is not likely to be helpful until the person in pain has expressed feelings with some assurance that he or she has been heard, understood, and accepted.

The transformation of overpowering and destructive emotions into positive, healthy emotions is not automatic, nor is it without painful inner struggles. The point to remember is this: feelings can be changed once they are claimed and taken seriously. The attentive and reflecting responses we discussed earlier help to emphasize the importance of claiming one's feelings and encouraging their expression.

HELPFUL RESPONSES TO
EXPRESSED FEELING

One type of response that can be helpful when strong feelings have been expressed is an identifying response. Identifying means indicating that you have had a similar feeling or experience, thus assuring people in crisis that they are being heard, understood, and accepted. However, caution is needed when you attempt to identify with what is being expressed. The helping process can be hindered when the conversation turns to your experience and feelings. Relating your own story tends to sidetrack the helping process by directing conversation away from the problem and feelings that are being shared by the person with a special need. These are examples of concise identifying statements:

- "Yes, I have felt that way before."
- "I know how it feels to be left out."
- "That same thing happened to me, and I felt like you do."
- "I think I would feel the same way if I'd been through what you have."

An identifying statement lets people know that they are being heard sympathetically, but does not shift attention to your own story—which could be heard as "I can top that" storytelling. It is surely appropriate to share your own story and insights with a person with whom you are building a relationship of mutual trust and warmth. Your own willingness to share your feelings and experiences can help to encourage expression on the part of another. The caution, however, is this: when a person who is hurting shares a significant level of feeling with you, relating your own story can easily be a means of running away from the painful feelings that have been exposed. Even if you are not aware of doing so, the one in pain will very easily detect any signs of flight on your part from the frightening emotional baggage he or she has shared with you. For this reason, some reflecting and exploring of feelings should usually precede identifying responses. (See "Helping Skills," listed in introduction.)

Confronting is another response that may be introduced after significant expression of feeling has taken place. In confrontation, you point out apparent conflicts or inconsistencies between words and actions, between another's perceptions and the reality of the situation. The purpose is to provide that person with an awareness that may be helpful to him or her. It is important to keep this purpose in mind as you use this technique because confrontation can also be a way of refuting or devaluing feelings, neither of which is helpful to the person who is hurting.

These are some examples of unhelpful ways to confront someone:

- "I don't see how you can say that after all your husband has done for you."
- "You say you feel put down but I've never heard anybody put you down."

- "All of your concern seems to be with what is happening to you. Don't you think it's time to think about someone else?"

Responses that pronounce judgment or depreciate the feelings of the person who is hurting should be avoided.

These are examples of helpful ways to confront someone:

- "You are expressing a lot of anxiety about this surgery, but your voice and face are completely placid. Is it pretty important to you to keep it all in?"
- "You keep saying you're not going to let this problem bother you, but you seem pretty angry about it. I wonder if you're really being honest with yourself."

The way in which you follow up a confronting statement is as important as the confrontation itself. You, as a helper, should be prepared to hear and accept whatever emotional reaction the confrontation triggers in the other person, whether it is sullen withdrawal or a flood of emotional outpouring. Usually further exploration and assurance that the confrontation was not a final assessment will be helpful. The more tentative the confrontation ("I wonder if . . .") and the more you identify with the feeling expressed ("I've felt pretty angry before without knowing why. Maybe that's what you're feeling."), the more likely it is that the person you want to help will accept the insight you offer.

An additional helping response to the person who expresses deep feelings is to test the accuracy of your perceptions. This can be done by summarizing the main themes you have heard the person express. The summary statement can be offered tentatively to allow the person to correct or add to it. Examples of testing statements:

- "Let me see if I understand you. You're more concerned about being alone than about the pain following surgery."
- "There seem to be two strong feelings going on at once—

anger at your wife for leaving you, and fear that she won't come back."

- "It sounds like you've identified some pretty heavy issues: your mother's illness, your husband's drinking problem, and your frustration with your job."

The purpose of the testing statement is to be sure you haven't misunderstood the feeling the person has been expressing. It ensures that you didn't miss something of consequence.

An important part of your response to the feelings the other person expresses is to avoid labeling what you are hearing. Labels such as "hostile," "bad," "good," or "paranoid" can get in the way of the helping process. A label is a name or descriptive word that has powerful emotional content because of its heavily negative connotations—especially for a person who is in crisis. Many people already feel overly exposed and vulnerable when they are sharing their feelings, and the use of emotionally charged words in response can stick to them like glue.

It is not always easy to know what words or phrases will have this kind of power over a person, so some exploration may be helpful. Examples of labeling and nonlabeling responses:

1. a. "So you've been pretty weak for the last few days." (labeling)
   b. "You've cried very easily for a few days now." (nonlabeling)

2. a. "I guess you've been hostile with everyone for the past few days." (labeling)
   b. "It sounds like you've felt a lot of anger recently, and several people around you have caught part of that." (nonlabeling)

Common sense can usually tell you what words tend to stick

with a person as a label. Even if you feel it fits, you should be aware of the reaction the label might trigger in the person who is hurting. It is important to use neutral words or words that are likely to have a positive connotation for that person. If there is any question in your mind about someone's reaction to a word or phrase you have used, it would be a good idea to ask. (Example: "Does 'terrified' sound a little too strong to you?")

As you hear and respond to the feelings of the person who is hurting, you may want to answer or resolve all the questions before the conversation ends. But for those going through a crisis in their lives, the ventilation of deep inner emotions may well be enough to expect in one conversation. The helping relationship may be greatly enhanced if you do not rush too quickly to provide answers and helpful suggestions. Very often the new experience of expressing strong feelings without being put down or rejected will be enough to require some time for adjustment. Like a child taking its first step, these feelings should be met with encouragement and affirmation rather than criticism.

As a helping person, you can give reassurance and acceptance by offering to do two things after you have been entrusted with these strong feelings:

1. Offer to pray about the hurts, fears, anxieties, or frustrations that have been expressed. If the person wants you to pray, offer to God the main emotional themes you have heard for the understanding, insight, and healing that only God can provide. Use very simple and direct language to commit these deeply personal concerns to God.

2. Suggest another time within the next few days when you could get together again. It might be a good idea to suggest that you will want to hear then how the person is feeling and to talk further about what he or she might do to get a different perspective on the situation or to alter the circumstances. A

definite time to meet again, combined with the hope of discovering some positive alternatives, may provide the measure of hope a person in crisis needs.

Your attentive listening to and reflecting of feelings, and the acceptance you offer can set the context for a person in crisis to move on to explore specific possibilities to cope with or resolve his or her crisis. But most important, your presence and personal involvement have given the person a message of acceptance and hope rather than rejection. This speaks of the very presence of a caring, loving God.

> "O Lord, the God who saves me,
>   day and night I cry out before you.
> May my prayer come before you;
>   turn your ear to my cry.
> For my soul is full of trouble
>   and my life draws near the grave.
> I am counted among those who go down to the pit;
>   I am like a man without strength."
>
> (Ps. 88:1–4)

NOTES

1. The training process outlined by Dennis Kinlaw in the training manual entitled *Helping Skills for Human Resource Development* (San Diego: University Associates, Inc., 1981) is recommended for use in training groups. The exercises contained in this manual take seriously the need to develop new patterns of response in order to assist a person in exploring and working through overpowering emotions.

2. Henri Nouwen, *The Living Reminder* (New York: Seabury Press, 1977), 22.

3

HOPELESSNESS AND DESPAIR

"All is not lost"

John and Louise had worked hard and planned carefully for their retirement. John had been a sales representative for a chemical firm, and Louise had worked for many years as a secretary and receptionist. They both dreamed of the time when they could travel and devote more time to their own interests. Their children and grandchildren lived in other states, and they planned to spend some time with them. It seemed their years of waiting and working and saving were about to be rewarded. Then, suddenly, their plans and dreams were shattered.

Without warning John had a severe heart attack. For several days it was not certain that he would even live. But gradually his condition improved. The expensive treatment during his prolonged period of recovery caused them to spend some of their hard-earned savings. Even after his release from the hospital, John was restricted to a limited diet and very little physical activity. His medicines and therapy continued to drain their limited financial reserves. Their plans to do some traveling were postponed indefinitely by John's physical disability and their dwindling funds.

During the time that John was in the hospital, Pastor Johnson and several of John and Louise's friends from the church were very concerned and supportive. When John was allowed to go home they brought food to the house and offered other kinds of assistance. After several weeks had passed and things seemed to be more normal for John and Louise, this contact with others dropped off considerably.

It was then that some of their friends noticed a change in them. Both Louise and John seemed withdrawn and sometimes even unfriendly. Offers to help were often met with a rebuff, such as, "Oh no, we don't want to be any trouble to you." And sometimes, in telephone conversations, John expressed the wish that he had not survived his heart attack. From time to time, Louise broke into tears while talking with friends, expressing deep concern about John's loss of the will to live. Louise herself seemed exhausted by their ordeal; some of those who knew her well were alarmed by an edge of bitterness that sometimes crept into her conversation.

A few of these Christian friends got together with the pastor and expressed their concern for John and Louise. Some of them were frustrated that their attempts to help were turned aside by either John or Louise. They asked the pastor, "What can we do for them?"

In the discussion that followed, as these concerned friends talked about their efforts to help, it became clear that John and Louise were walling themselves off from the relationships and activities that had always been most meaningful to them. With that puzzling realization came the awareness that John and Louise had lost hope. Life for them had lost its purpose because some important things they had been living for were no longer possible now. They felt empty, betrayed, and bitter about their situation. They felt that God had deserted them, and they even wondered if they were being punished by God for something they had done. The one word that best described what John and Louise felt was hopelessness.

LOSING HOPE

Hopes, dreams, and plans give meaning and direction to life. The need for purposeful and compelling goals is basic to mankind. Dr. Viktor Frankl, in his book entitled *Man's Search for Meaning*,[1] tells of the crucial difference goals played for Jews in the Nazi concentration camps during World War II. For many of the people Dr. Frankl was imprisoned with, survival of the most horrible conditions was made possible by the fact that they had compelling goals that gave meaning even to their suffering. Hopes and dreams have incredible motivating power. They provide us with the incentive we need to overcome setbacks or handicaps, to grow through suffering, and to make positive contributions even when life seems hostile and unfair.

When hopes are dashed, so is the motivation we need to live with a sense of meaning or purpose. To paraphrase an old truth, When there is no hope the people perish. As with John and Louise, the loss of major goals in life often results in withdrawal from others and a deep sense of emptiness, despair, even bitterness. There are countless tragic events that shatter hopes and dreams; the most common feeling that results from these shattering events is hopelessness.

Hopelessness comes from the loss of an important goal that gave meaning to the life of a person. It is a common and powerful experience when a specific goal or plan is lost. But there is an important difference between the loss of hope, which is specific, and the kind of hopelessness that is general and inclusive, seeming to encompass all of one's life.

Despair combines the deep feeling that all of life has lost its meaning and feelings of powerlessness and resignation. It is the result of *all* hopes being lost to a person. Since there is nothing left in life that offers consolation or encouragement, the dominant feeling is "All is lost!" Bitterness, apathy, or withdrawal may signal the beginning of despair, but the desire to die is the strongest evidence of its presence.

There is both an emotional and spiritual dimension to the

state of despair. A person in despair may feel abandoned and rejected by God, as the cry of the Psalmist reveals:

> "Why, O Lord, do you reject me
>   and hide your face from me?
> From my youth I have been afflicted and
>   close to death;
>   I have suffered your terrors and am in despair.
> Your wrath has swept over me;
>   your terrors have destroyed me.
> All day long they surround me like a flood;
>   they have completely engulfed me.
> You have taken my companions and loved ones
>   from me;
>   the darkness is my closest friend."
>
> (Ps. 88:14–18)

The sense of loss many people experience is so complete and consuming that they often ask the questions "Where is God?" or even "Is there a God?" Even though there may be many things left to give meaning to their lives, people in despair *feel* that all is lost. In spite of the fact that God is with them, they do not experience the comfort of God's presence or the hope for the future that God provides.

The question of God's whereabouts is best answered by actions rather than words. Attempts to persuade those who have lost hope that all is not lost are apt to be futile. Your explanations will simply confirm for them that you do not understand the depth of their loss. Your values may differ from theirs to such an extent that a devastating loss for them may seem unimportant to you. The question for you, the helper, is whether you are willing to invest yourself in their pain and frustration long enough so that they are, in fact, touched by the God who cares in the midst of hopelessness. An even more basic question is, Is *your* faith strong enough to experience their pain and loss without yourself losing sight of God's loving presence? It isn't easy, but then who said it's supposed to be?

MAKING CONTACT

The first crucial step in helping John and Louise, or anyone who feels hopeless, is the difficult task of making contact. It is important that close friends be willing to take the initiative, even though those initiatives may be repeatedly rebuffed. Simple things like a phone call, a ride to a church activity, or an invitation to the home of a friend played an important part in letting John and Louise know that they were still important to their friends. When they turned down an invitation they were assured that it was okay this time but their friends would be calling again.

After several weeks of unintrusive but persistent attention from a few friends and occasional visits by their pastor, Louise asked one of her friends to talk with her about "our predicament."

"I just felt like no one could help," Louise told her. "But I have to be able to talk with someone. I guess I don't feel that I have a right to burden anyone else with our problems."

First Louise, and then John, began to express the shock, the anger, and the hopelessness they felt. They were ready to move forward from despair into a process of mourning what they had lost. Their Christian friends were allowed to help them with that process because those friends had been willing to work at the task of making contact and staying in touch with John and Louise during their time of crisis.

This is not an easy task since many of us are conditioned, by the individualism and privacy in our culture, to leave people alone whenever they withdraw. When offers to help are turned away, it is common for friends—even in the church—to say, "All right. I tried, and they weren't interested. You just see if I offer to help again! I'll just mind my own business!" The withdrawal of those who are in great pain is met with withdrawal on the part of those who have tried to help. This alienation, and the feeling it stirs within us, often leaves us with deep wounds that separate friends and diminish the healing power of the church as a caring community.

The solution to this problem is neither simple nor easy. It requires an understanding of the pain felt by those who have suffered a serious loss; it requires patience to keep reaching out, even when the offers are not accepted. It is a risky business to hang in there, to keep going back until the time is right. But our model is Christ. In fact, going back after your previous attempts have been rejected bears powerful witness to the depth of concern you have for the person who is looking for some hopeful sign.

I am not suggesting that you should insist upon helping against people's wishes. Nor would I suggest that you demand to be the *one* to help; that is merely egotism. But the grace to keep reaching out a helping hand in an unobtrusive and non-pushy way is a discipline that often bears fruit, sometimes after many months. That is the difference between God's redemptive love and our human attempts to love!

MOURNING WHAT IS LOST

When we hear the words *grief* and *mourning,* scenes of funerals and cemeteries often come to mind. But there are many losses in life other than death that also call for a process of grief and mourning:

- The middle-aged man who faces permanent disability after an accident
- The young wife whose husband has left her with two small children to rear
- The parents of a child who has leukemia

- The aging wife whose husband of forty years has had a
  stroke and requires constant nursing care

These are only a few examples of losses that produce a grief
reaction. All of these people have lost something crucial in
their lives. Mourning that loss is necessary for them to make
the most of their circumstances. Unless that task of mourning
is completed, these people will be crippled in their ability to
embrace any new plans or possibilities for their lives.

The primary skills required to assist those who are going
through this grieving process vary according to the stage of the
grief process in which each person is involved.[2] During the
early stages of mourning, the skills of inviting the expression of
feelings, acknowledging what has been expressed, active listening, reflecting, and testing will be most helpful. At this point
the emphasis should be on listening and encouraging expression, without much evaluation or rebuttal.

The main challenge in the early stages of mourning is to actually feel the pain experienced by people in crisis, and then to
carry that pain into the presence of God in prayer for healing.
It may require some effort on your part to listen to and identify
with anger toward God, anger toward more fortunate acquain-
tances (even yourself), and bitterness about life's unfairness,
without going on the defensive. (Actually, does God need to be
defended?) Yet, if you feel defensive, it will keep your relationship on an honest level if you acknowledge that you feel a little
threatened by what is being expressed.

In the later stages of the grief process, you can use the skills
of testing the accuracy of your perceptions, identifying
resources that may be helpful in making the adjustment, and
suggesting alternatives they might explore. Even the suggestion of alternative ways of looking at the situation may be
helpful as your friends move through their feelings of loss.
Finally, they will be ready to do some action planning to ex-

plore, with your help, what realistic goals and dreams they can now set for themselves.

It is not possible to set a definite time frame for the mourning process. People and circumstances vary drastically. But as a general rule, the more traumatic the loss the longer it will take to let go emotionally of what has been lost. It will take several months, or even years, to recover from catastrophic losses. A strong commitment of time and energy may be needed to stay with a person who is going through that adjustment.

Frequently, people who are working through the adjustment to such a loss will express embarrassment that they are not "snapping out of it" more quickly. They will often be caught off guard by waves of sorrow or anger, even after months of steady progress. What they need at such times is the reassurance from you that these emotional setbacks are a normal part of the process they are going through. It may also be very helpful to them if you assure them that you are willing to stay with them no matter how long it takes for them to regain their emotional equilibrium and zest for living. Fear that those providing support will get tired of the whole process can cause people who are grieving to keep their feelings to themselves, thus slowing the necessary emotional adjustment to their loss.

There are various signs that may indicate someone is not making a healthy adjustment to a loss. For example:

- Angry preoccupation with the irresponsibility of a former spouse, long after a divorce has been made final
- Complete concentration of attention on a terminally ill child by its mother, while neglecting the needs of other children
- Unwillingness to dispose of the personal effects of a spouse months after the funeral
- Bitter tirades, long after a loss has occurred, against those who are more fortunate

Any of these may indicate that a person is not making progress toward healthy emotional adjustment. A tactful confrontation from a trusted friend will sometimes be enough to move them out of the emotional rut in which they are caught. Even this type of confrontation, though, should be offered tentatively and without labels like "morbid preoccupation" or "child neglect."

There are times when professional counseling may be needed. You should be alert for signs that professional medical or counseling assistance may be required. Some signs that indicate a serious problem:

- A sustained loss of appetite with an accompanying weight loss
- Persistent sleeplessness and fatigue
- Prolonged periods of withdrawal and excessive sleeping
- Sudden changes in personality or personal habits and associations
- Talk about suicide or loss of the will to live

When any of these signs appear and persist, it is wise to consult your pastor or another professional regarding the most appropriate steps to take. If professional counseling or medical treatment is needed, it should be suggested to the person by someone whose judgment he or she trusts. It may be helpful if the person who suggests counseling can share the personal experience of a talk with a pastor or other counselor that proved to be helpful.

It is not uncommon for people to deny the loss they have experienced. Denial can take as many forms as there are people, but a few examples might help:

- A widow who still talks about her husband in the present tense, months after his death ("Fred enjoys baseball.")
- A father whose son is terminally ill but who still makes plans for his son's college years

- A young person suffering permanent paralysis who insists he or she is going to walk again some day

If you have established a significant level of trust with a person who is clearly denying a loss, a gentle and sympathetic reflection of the denial might be most helpful: "It sounds like you're wishing pretty hard that Jimmy would be able to go to college. I'm wishing that myself." Even such a gentle confrontation may be met by an angry response, however, so you should be prepared to respond with understanding to such reactions. An honest expression of your own feeling may allow you to say, "I'm on your side," without backing away from the painful reality you have pointed out. For example: "I truly wish Fred were still alive, too. I really miss him" or "Yes, I pray that a miracle will allow you to walk again, too."

There is a common misconception at this point that must be confronted. Very often those closest to a person who has lost a loved one (especially a husband, wife, or child) feel that they shouldn't mention the person who has died in the presence of the bereaved. They seem to feel that it would be painful for a spouse or parent to be reminded of their loss. When the mere mention of the deceased loved one brings tears to the eyes of the bereaved person, this only serves to confirm this feeling. There are two important points to be made: 1) Talking about a deceased or divorced spouse is an important part of emotionally accepting the loss of that loved one, and 2) The expression of sorrow among friends is a healthy thing that should elicit support rather than embarrassment. In fact, many widows, widowers and victims of divorce express frustration with friends who avoid conversation about the lost spouse. There are many rich memories connected with a loved one who has died, and those memories should be cherished rather than ignored in the course of adjusting to a loss.

It takes commitment and patience to help people through

the mourning process. Emotional setbacks can be discouraging to you, and periods of withdrawal might tempt you to leave your friends on their own. Since restoration requires a slow process of letting go of what has been lost, both the steadfast relationship you offer mourners and your willingness to experience their pain play key roles in their recovery. Listening deeply, responsively, prayerfully, and without judgment will provide the support that they need in order to accept what life still has to offer them.

ACCEPTING WHAT IS LEFT

As John and Louise were encouraged to express their anguish and allowed their friends to provide emotional support, they began to realize that there were still many important goals left worth pursuing. They had each other, their home, children and grandchildren, friends and neighbors, and many interests they could share. Although their physical activities were limited, they could still be involved in things they enjoyed. Fortunately Louise was able to work parttime in a friend's business. This extra income helped provide funds for a few trips they planned to take in the future.

This growing awareness of "all is not lost" did not come all at once. It came very gradually while they worked through their deep sense of loss and their anxiety about the future. Increasingly as time went on, they expressed appreciation to their friends and their pastor for seeing them through the dark days of anguish and grief.

It seems that in the economy of the human spirit, old dreams and obsolete plans must be discarded, however painfully, to make room for a fresh experience of life. To put it in Christian terms: death is followed by resurrection. Even when it seems that all is lost, there is still something left to embrace in life.

Even in the face of death the Christian has a hope that transcends the finality of the grave:

Who shall separate us from the love of Christ?
Shall trouble or hardship or persecution or famine
   or nakedness or danger or sword?
As it is written:
   "For your sake we face death all day long;
   we are considered as sheep to be slaughtered."
No, in all these things we are more than conquerors
   through him who loved us.
For I am convinced that neither death nor life,
   neither angels nor demons, neither the present
   nor the future, nor any powers, neither height
   nor depth, nor anything else in all creation, will
   be able to separate us from the love of God that is
   in Christ Jesus our Lord.

                                       (Rom. 8:35–39)

This is not a denial of the pain and loss that accompany tragedy and death; rather, it is a reminder that even the most tragic circumstances do not rob life of meaning. What is the difference? It is God's redemptive love which each of us is called to embody with those who are passing through the deep waters of pain, loneliness, sorrow, and loss. By listening and praying and staying through the dark days of hopelessness and despair, you earn the right to participate in the recovery of hope and the rebuilding of life.

HELPFUL RESPONSES

There are several helping skills that can be employed to aid people in the exploration and discovery of what life has yet to offer those who have been hurt. Your purpose as a helper should not be to set goals, but to serve as a source of encouragement and to help test the realism of their hopes and dreams, a vitally important need for many who struggle to regain a hold on life.

The skills of probing and testing can help identify basic values or commitments in the lives of people who have been hurt. The deeper values and dreams that gave meaning to their lives are not always immediately obvious to them, but with patient exploration you can help to identify those commitments and motivations that are solid enough to support the recovery of their dreams and hopes. Probing questions can help them clarify and develop the unique set of needs, desires, and abilities that will form the basis of the life they must now build for themselves.

Examples of probing responses:

- "What can you do with your hands that you've enjoyed doing before?"
- "If you're not able to travel abroad as you've planned, are there still some shorter and less expensive trips you'd like to take?"
- "Have you given some thought to the things you'd like to do with your life, now that you are alone?"

Examples of testing responses:

- "How important to you is it that you stay in this house now that you can't take care of the yard by yourself?"
- "Is your desire to get your degree strong enough to carry you through two years of classes?"
- "You said you'd like to volunteer at the hospital. Will you have the time and energy to do that?"

There may be times when your probing or testing elicits a hostile or negative response from the person recovering from a major loss. When that happens it is important to back off slightly and explore what the person is feeling. Your own common sense can usually allow you to distinguish between unhealthy resistance to constructive suggestions on the one hand, and an indication that he or she is not yet ready to move forward on the other hand. Even a negative response gives you useful information about the person's readiness to take action.

One friend helped John realize that he had always longed for the time to study the fascinating field of astronomy. That was something John had the time to do now, and he began to set some goals for himself in that area. Louise came to recognize that she had always been too busy to get as well acquainted with her neighbors as she would have liked, so she began making plans to get together. These discoveries encouraged them both to continue exploring and dreaming about what was still possible for them.

It is not uncommon for those who have been through a time of mourning to try to make up for lost time once they begin to get a new taste of life. They may try to do more than they can reasonably hope to accomplish. The skills of tactfully confronting and challenging unrealistic goals or expectations can be a very important part of the helping relationship at this point. These challenges are made to test the reality of the new hopes and expectations. This may seem to be a thankless task, but it is important to help these people who are recovering from a major loss to avoid yet another one. Realistic recognition of their limitations now is as important to their recovery as the rediscovery of possibilities. It is not your responsibility to set these limitations for them—in fact, people have a way of surprising you with what they can manage—but it is responsible and caring to challenge the realism of a new course of action.

From the dreaming and goal-setting process you may encourage the more specific task of planning for action. An action plan should include as many details as possible that relate to the accomplishment of a particular goal. It should include an estimate of the time, money, and energy required to accomplish each step of the plan. This allows those making the plan to commit themselves to action rather than ideas. The action plan should be flexible enough to allow for change but definite enough to provide a guide toward a particular goal.

As you help people recovering from a major loss, you should

be aware of the lingering and permanent effects of the loss they have experienced. Like a body recovering from major surgery, they may have less ability to cope with setbacks and frustrations for some time. They may become more easily defeated and slip back into feeling, "It's no use!" Usually a little encouragement and support at these times will help them get through. Sometimes, though, they may simply need to rest for a while in order to regroup and try again.

Clearly the time when hopes and dreams are being rebuilt is not as demanding on the helper as is the period of mourning a major loss. Yet even as the joyful process of rebuilding is taking place, you should keep in mind the special needs of those who have been deeply hurt. There are many losses in life that people do not ever completely get over, and it would be unrealistic to expect those who have experienced such a loss to act as though it never happened. (For example, someone who has lost a spouse after many years of marriage.) But with your help and understanding they can overcome many of the negative effects of their loss and even make their wounds of the past a source of healing for others who are hurting.

Just as you have encouraged people to open their pain and anguish to God's healing power, it is appropriate to encourage them to bring their gratitude and celebration to God. Those who have experienced the grace of God at the very brink of despair can be a source of great blessing and encouragement to those who are going through difficult and painful passages in life as well.

> "Unless the Lord has given me help,
>   I would soon have dwelt in the silence of death.
> When I said, 'My foot is slipping,'
>   Your love, O Lord, supported me.
> When anxiety was great within me,
>   Your consolation brought joy to my soul."
>   (Ps. 94:17–19)

NOTES

1. Viktor Frankl, *Man's Search for Meaning* (Boston: Beacon Press, 1962).

2. Elisabeth Kübler-Ross, *On Death and Dying* (New York: Macmillan, 1969), 34–159.

4

HELPLESSNESS

"You can still help yourself"

Those who have suffered a major loss or physical breakdown
will often say things like, "What can I do?" or "Nothing I do
makes any difference." With these statements they are expressing feelings of helplessness that often run very deep. This feeling of helplessness is coupled very closely with the sense of
hopelessness; they go hand in hand. While with hopelessness
there is a lack of any clear vision for the future, helplessness involves an inability to take any action to bring a positive change
in the painful circumstances in which they are caught. A loss
of hope usually precedes and helps create the feeling of helplessness.

In the case of physical illness or disability, there may be the
loss of some of the ability to perform even very simple tasks.
Those who suffer a stroke, heart attack, or spinal injury may
suffer a permanent loss of functional ability. When they recall
their previous physical abilities, it seems to them that there are
no worthwhile activities left for them.

In a similar way those who suffer painful losses, through
divorce, the loss of a job, or the death of a spouse, may feel
helpless to bring any order or meaning to their lives. The emotional impact of such a loss may be completely immobilizing.
It is almost impossible for those who are going through such a
crisis to distinguish between their actual limitations and their
feeling of helplessness.

Whether the crisis is physical, emotional, or both, people

who are going through it need the help of others with even
very simple and routine tasks like eating, bathing, and
remembering to pay the bills. Family members and professional personnel in hospitals and convalescent centers do for
them what they cannot do for themselves.

It is usually difficult, however, for those who are helping to
know how much they should do for someone suffering an illness, injury, or loss. For each person that healthy balance between independence and dependence comes at a different
point. An eighty-two-year-old stroke victim with right-side
paralysis will be much more dependent than a twenty-five-
year-old accident victim with paralysis below the waist. The
question of how much to do for a person depends upon how
much that person should be able to do for him- or herself.

During the acute phase of a physical or emotional crisis, it is
appropriate for those who are helping to do a lot of things for
people that they would normally be able to do for themselves.
But, especially during an acute crisis, those who offer help
often do more than is necessary. This can be a genuine expression of loving concern, and there is nothing wrong with it.
Your taking over may help those who need help recognize they
are not alone in their pain and loss: "Bear one another's
burdens and so fulfill the law of Christ . . ." (Gal. 6:2). The
recovery process may even be accelerated when the normal
load is shared during a crisis.

When the acute crisis stage passes, however, it becomes increasingly important to encourage people to do more for themselves. This does not mean you should leave them alone;
rather, careful attention should be given to increase their level
of independence. After suffering a severe loss or disability,
people may need a lot of help just to recognize that there are
still things they can do for themselves. Your support can be the
vital link that enables them to come to that realization. It may

take a lot of time and energy, but you can help. "For everyone has to carry his own load" (Gal. 6:5).

LIFE WITHIN LIMITS

All of our lives are lived within limits, and our potential is developed within those limits. In one way or another we all ask the question, "What is it possible for me to do with my life?" The process of maturing involves a continual exploration of how much or how little control we have over our own destiny. We live our lives in a field of forces; some we can influence while others are completely beyond our control.

Our potential and our limits are shaped for us by three main factors in our lives:

1. Our biological heritage is the baseline that sets limits on our lives. Such important factors as physical strength, height, facial features, body type, motor coordination, agility, and, to some degree, our intellectual ability and emotional sensitivity are all part of our biological heritage. We have little or no control over these natural limits, though we do have a strong influence on how we develop the potential we are given.

2. Our social environment also plays a strong role in setting our limits. The kind of care we receive from our early years through adolescence is crucial in shaping our ability to love and be loved in later years. The values we learn, the rewards and punishment we receive, the religious training we are given, all mold the moral and ethical boundaries within which we live. The mental and physical stimulation we receive, the expectations of others, our economic status, and scores of other social factors shape and limit our potential development. These influences form the context within which our vision of ourselves and our world is formed. Our choices are made within the boundaries we have inherited.

3. Our personal responses are the crucial third dimension in our development as individuals. Given our particular biolog-

ical and social heritage, there are many choices we have to make that shape and control our own identity. The intangible inner qualities we call attitude, will, and character play powerfully important roles in shaping and defining our options in life. These personal qualities are formed from the social and biological raw materials we are given.

The interaction of these three forces forms our identity within the limits that are set for us. From them, we form our own understanding of who we are and what kind of world we live in. Few of us ever attain our physical or mental potential. We make our "deal" with life, and the identity we arrive at is the footing upon which we stand to face life's challenges.

Whether we see ourselves as smart or dull, aggressive or passive, clumsy or graceful, strong or weak, the identity we adopt provides us with the type of security we feel we need. We may wish we were rich or tall, but we can usually come to terms with reality when we settle for being barely solvent or less than ideally proportioned. In order to accept reality we must discard many dreams that are beyond our reach. So the words "I can't" may become a way of defending ourselves against unrealistic or undesirable expectations and of protecting the identity we claim for ourselves.

THE LONG ROAD TO
RECOVERY

Dave and Donna were happily married, in their early thirties, and enthusiastic about life. They were active in their church; both had satisfying jobs and many good friends. They had a five-year-old son Jimmy who was happy and healthy. They owned their own home and lived life fully until one rainy night when a drunken driver crossed over the center line and hit their car head on.

Dave, Donna, and Jimmy were taken to the hospital emergency room by ambulance. Jimmy's injuries were the least serious—a broken collarbone and lacerations. Donna, with head and back injuries, was unconscious. She was placed in traction in the intensive care area. Dave had suffered massive internal injuries and was taken immediately into surgery. But despite the best efforts of the medical team, Dave died on the operating table.

Their parents and their pastor were called to the hospital, where they maintained a vigil with Jimmy while Donna hovered between life and death. Three days passed before Donna gradually began to regain consciousness. The reality of Dave's death came to her very slowly, after which she experienced periods of tearful depression followed by acute concern about Jimmy. After a week the family made Dave's funeral arrangements with Donna, but the memorial service was held without Donna or Jimmy. Jimmy was allowed to visit Donna after about ten days, and soon he was released to go home with Donna's parents.

Donna was in a lot of pain—physically and emotionally—and had to undergo a series of operations to repair her neck and back injuries. Six weeks after the accident she was able to sit up for the first time and she soon began an active physical therapy program that lasted for more than two months before she returned home. During this time in the hospital, Donna's pastor and a hospital chaplain visited her regularly. They helped her work through her deep grief over Dave's death as they listened and prayed with her. Donna's good friend, Barb, also came to visit twice a week. These visits were times Donna looked forward to, and the friendship between Donna and Barb deepened. They laughed and wept together, and Barb helped Donna by running errands, contacting friends, and handling many small but important details.

Nearly four months after the accident Donna was able to go home. She knew she would have some permanent disability due to her back injury, but she was able to walk, although with some difficulty, and do some light activities. Her mother stayed with her and helped take care of Jimmy, while Barb continued spending some time each week helping with errands and housework. Barb listened and offered support when Donna was discouraged and depressed. They would talk about how good life had been when Dave was alive and how frightened Donna now felt about trying to rear Jimmy by herself. Barb often assured Donna that she would stand by her through whatever lay ahead, and Donna expressed deep appreciation for Barb's loyal friendship.

As Donna continued to progress physically, she still allowed her parents and Barb to do what they were willing to do to help her. She did not try to do much with Jimmy, and she declined invitations to do things with her friends. A few times she commented that she did not want to be a burden to anyone, saying, "No one needs a widow with a bad back around." When her mother asked Donna one day if she could take more responsibility for Jimmy's care, Donna responded defensively with, "Well, I guess you'd have to go through what I've been through to understand that I'm doing all I can."

Nearly a year after the accident, Barb and other friends knew that Donna was refusing to do much of what she could be doing for herself and Jimmy. Some of these friends began backing away to let Donna fend more for herself. One day as Barb was helping Donna with some housework, Donna told her that she felt hurt because some of her friends as well as her own mother had pulled away from her. She described them as cold and unsympathetic. "They act as if it's my fault that this happened to me," she said. "If I could help it I would, but I can't! What do they expect of me, anyway?" With that she burst into tears.

Barb tried to console her, but Donna insisted that people just expected too much from her. As they talked, Barb asked Donna what she expected from herself. Donna replied, "I really can't do anything. I can't bend over to help Jimmy. I can't stand up for very long at one time. I can't walk without a limp. I don't even have a husband to help me! And there's nothing I can do to change the situation."

Later, as Barb thought about that conversation, she realized she was not willing to accept Donna's helplessness. Several times she tried to talk with Donna about what she could still do, if she wanted to, to become more independent. Each time Donna put her off with "Yes, but . . ." statements until Barb stopped suggesting alternatives.

Donna had lost much of the identity she had established before the accident. Her roles as wife, mother, and busy, active woman were all shattered at once. In place of the identity she had previously known, there was that of accident victim and widow. No longer able to do what had once given meaning to her life, she felt that she could do nothing. It was only natural to depend on those who were willing to do things for her. Recalling and reminding others of her loss and injury became a way of defending her victim status.

Before her accident and loss, Donna had an identity with which she was very happy. She had learned to be a good wife to Dave and a good mother to Jimmy. She managed the household, did the housework and gardening, prepared meals, and carried out hundreds of other tasks. This active lifestyle gave her a sense of accomplishment. She saw herself as an energetic, friendly, and intelligent person with a lot to offer. She gave little thought to the things she could *not* do with her life.

The accident changed all that. Dave's death and her painful back injury shattered two vital components of her identity—wife and mother. The frustration of being disabled while Jimmy recovered from his injuries magnified her loss. Her identity was taken away from her by events and circumstances she could not control.

Donna mourned not only Dave's death but also the parts of her own identity she had lost. The familiar pattern of activities that had given her a sense of control over her own life was lost to her. But during the time of recuperation, in the hospital and at home, she was developing a new identity without being aware of it. Her life had been so radically changed by the accident that she had come to see herself primarily as a victim. With this new identity as a victim came the inner conviction that she was helpless to do much about her situation. Some of her friends felt that she was simply indulging in self-pity when they heard her refer frequently to the accident as the main reality in her life—even many months after it had happened. But as Barb listened, she realized that Donna was not just feeling sorry for herself. She recognized that some of Donna's self-pity and dependency was her way of coping with a painful new set of realities. By encouraging Donna to express her feelings of hopelessness and helplessness, Barb helped Donna work through her grief over what she had lost. Gradually, Barb was able to challenge her to look at what she could still do for herself and for others.

At first Donna's response to these challenges was defensive, sometimes even abrasive. Eventually Donna and Barb began to explore together what possibilities still existed—activities, plans, and hopes. As her physical therapy progressed, Donna realized that she could begin doing some of the tasks she had avoided. She began to assume more responsibility for Jimmy's care and to do some light housework. With the support of Barb, Donna began to rebuild her life within a new set of limitations.

HELPFUL RESPONSES

There are several skills that you as a helper can use to encourage those who are feeling helpless in the face of pain and loss. Your primary goal is to assist them in identifying and mobilizing the resources available to them that will enable them to overcome the loss or injury they have sustained. The assistance you offer should be aimed at supporting their efforts to help themselves.

A vivid example of this principle at work may be seen with persons who become blind. You can offer to bring things to them; you can read what they need to know to them. But it is much more helpful to these people if you can teach them to read Braille and to move around to find things for themselves. Of course, immediate needs must be met, but the real goal of a helping relationship is to foster independence.

The responsive listening skills of reflecting, probing, and exploring are helpful as you focus on the person's feelings about what has been lost. Exploring skills can be particularly helpful in the search for previously developed functions and identity, and determining what parts of it are now actually lost. The strongest feelings people express are clues that can lead you to the most painful areas of loss in their life.

The skill of problem-stating can be used effectively to bring to the surface the specific areas in which people feel helpless to act. If they are going to be able to take action to help themselves, it is important that they claim their feelings of resignation. The more specifically the problem can be identified, the more likely it is that a specific action plan can be developed to overcome it. Examples of problem-stating responses:

1. "Let me see if I understand the problem you're facing. You have always taken pride in your athletic ability, but now you feel you can't do anything athletic."

2. "I realize that many of the activities that you have always thrived on are no longer possible for you. Now it is a challenge to find some things you can do that can take their place."

The skill of tactful confrontation can be a valuable tool in pointing out ways a person may be hanging on to a victim identity. It is important when confronting to communicate respect for the feelings of the person you are confronting. A tentative statement leaves room for both of you to retreat gracefully. The valuable insight gained from à confrontation very often comes later as the person thinks about it privately. So if he or she is not pushed to immediately accept the suggestion you offer, the likelihood may be greater that the person will give it some thought without being defensive. An example of a confrontation that leaves the door open is "I wonder if you may be telling yourself you can't ever drive again as a way of avoiding a frightening responsibility."

Once people are engaged in the process of searching for options again, the skill of identifying resources available to them may be most helpful. It is important to be as specific as possible when selecting resources. Some testing may be necessary to determine their openness to the particular resource you suggest. For example: "How would you feel about joining a support group for divorced people that meets at the church each week?"

Identifying personal strengths at someone's disposal may be as important as finding outside resources. For example: "You know you have always been able to meet people easily and make a good impression. I wonder how you could make that work for you now?"

Planning for action is the next step in the helping process. The plan you develop together, though, must belong to your friend rather than to you. He or she must choose the plan's specific steps and they must be within his or her control. You can help by ensuring that the plan is realistic and encouraging your friend as he or she puts the plan in action.

While a plan of action is being tried, your role as a helper can be the supportive one of affirmation and encouragement.

There are likely to be setbacks even in a very good action plan. Your follow-up with people who are rebuilding their lives can be vital in their task of overcoming the problems they encounter. You can also be a part of the celebration when their accomplishments show progress toward overcoming a crisis or loss.

Barb's presence and availability gave Donna the encouragement she needed to build a new identity for herself. It was years before Donna felt secure in her ability to cope with the realities of her life, but five years after the accident she said this:

> "Right after the accident my friends and my pastor really gave me the courage to live. I felt so helpless when I thought of taking care of Jimmy and myself without Dave. I guess I just didn't see any real options for me.
>
> "My friends did a million things to help, but I guess they didn't know quite how to cope with my self-pity. Sometimes they would suggest things I could do, but I didn't feel like they were worth trying. No one enjoys being around someone who is feeling sorry for herself.
>
> "It seems like I didn't really begin to live again until my close friend Barb let me know that she expected more of me than I was expecting of myself. She helped me begin believing that I still had something very worthwhile to give to life—especially to Jimmy. It made a big difference to realize that there were still people who needed me.
>
> "I guess a lot of people had about given up on me after the first year. It looked like I might just be a helpless and depressing invalid the rest of my life. But I thank God for giving me someone like Barb, who believed in me even when I didn't believe in myself, someone who expected more out of me than years of self-pity."

THE PROBLEM OF
SECONDARY GAIN

You have no doubt met people who seem to thrive on a victim identity. They may move from one crisis to another, telling others about their predicaments in order to get some attention. It can be very frustrating to get involved in a helping relationship with these people, when whatever time and effort you spend seems to make little or no positive difference.

Those who study human behavior refer to a pattern that is often seen by those in the helping professions—doctors, nurses, social workers, ministers, and counselors. This pattern is referred to as "secondary gain," which means that an illness or other personal crisis is used to get attention and concern that may not be available otherwise. Very often the person who employs this pattern is not aware of it, but is attempting to meet hidden needs by this means.

A victim identity serves two main purposes for those who are hurting: it protects them from having too much expected of them ("Can't you see I'm not up to it?") and it secures for them a degree of caring attention of which they are usually not aware. Nor are the crises phony or made-up, though there may be a tendency to exaggerate pain or loss to a level sufficient to require attention ("Can't you see how I'm struggling?"). This pattern may work well until those who help get tired of the recurring crises that demand their attention.

If you are highly motivated to help those in distress, you may attract any number of people who thrive on crisis attention. These relationships can be mutually satisfying and meet needs for you as well as for the people in distress. However, when the good feeling of being needed disintegrates into a feeling of being used, then it is only natural that you find yourself pulling back to protect yourself.

While this response may make it clear to those in crisis that they must carry their own load, it is also likely to convince them that the next time they must have an even more serious problem to merit your continued attention. There will inevitably come a point at which their burdens are just too much for you to carry. There are several ways this relationship can become destructive for both of you:

- When you become impatient with the unwillingness on the part of victims to take action to help themselves
- When you try to help victims in a way they don't want to be helped
- When victims refuse to take responsibility for their unwise choices and actions that bring more trouble
- When victims demand more of your time and energy than you want to give
- When you begin to resent carrying responsibilities for victims that they could carry themselves

Obviously, it is just as unhelpful to reject those who cling to a victim identity as it is to make demands on them or accuse them of not doing their fair share. If you find yourself caught in this kind of destructive relationship, you are confronted with a very difficult dilemma: to keep trying to help and risk being used, or to back away and leave the victim feeling hurt and rejected.

Several questions may help to clarify whether or not secondary gain is being used by the victim within a helping relationship:

- Is there any evidence that the symptoms or pain are being exaggerated? Is there an obvious attempt to elicit sympathy by dramatizing the suffering?
- Are requests for help appropriate? Are these requests for aid things that can be done by the person? ("Would you please call my brother and ask him to come and see me?")

- Are your suggestions of resources or options met with resistance? ("Yes, but . . .") Is it more important to *you* than it is to the person that he or she improve?
- Does the conversation center on problems, hurt, and symptoms, leaving little room for more positive subjects (plans, hopes, dreams, other people)? Does the person define him- or herself only in terms of needs, weaknesses and pain rather than strengths, possibilities and assets?
- Do most of the person's relationships derive from, or center on, his or her problem, injury, loss, or hurt?

If the answers make it clear that a person is deriving a lot of secondary gain from being a victim, a more difficult question arises: how can you help without playing into an unhealthy pattern of manipulation? This person does need help, but it may be very difficult to give it without fostering and rewarding a victim role. If it is very important to you to be the rescuer, you must accept the risks of that relationship. The time and energy you expend in trying to help may be rewarded with little or no lasting progress.

It may help to recognize at the outset that the victim is simply trying to meet very legitimate needs for attention, respect, and love. It is the *method* he or she uses that gets in the way. And the method may be very difficult to give up. These people need your understanding, patience, and acceptance as much as anyone else does. Any challenge or call for them to change their style should come only after you have established a trusting relationship by listening and responding to their feelings.

It is important that you set some realistic limits in the helping relationship, however. Though it is often difficult to say no to those you deeply care about, especially when they are hurting, it is necessary to do so in order to establish clear expectations. For example:

- "I know this house is awfully empty, but I do need to be

with my own family tonight."
- "I'm really not able to see you every day, but I will come as often as I can."

You may need to seek the advice of someone whose training and insights you trust to check out how realistic limits may be set, since it is often impossible to accurately and objectively assess the appropriateness of the requests and expectations of one who is hurting.

When you have a warm relationship with the person with a victim identity, an honest discussion of your relationship can help to clarify mutual expectations. Such a discussion could begin with a clear statement from you, such as, "I want to help you get through this time, but I don't want to get in the way by doing things or making decisions for you that you are capable of making for yourself."

A tactful confrontation may also be helpful: "Several times now you've brought up a big problem to talk about, but when I've asked about your hopes or plans you don't seem to want to talk about that. Is it possible that you're shutting yourself off from some things you could be doing to help yourself?" Such an intervention—well timed—can develop a whole new area of understanding for that person, though it may be painful to accept at first. In most cases it is important to back off without arguing or defending your suggestion, though a further confrontation could be to point out the defensive reaction your suggestion brings.

An exploration of new possibilities can be a very rewarding way of helping a person to give up a victim style. Though it is often difficult to accurately assess possibilities in the midst of a crisis, a question such as, "What can you change in this situation?" can help focus attention on the fact that there is usually something that can be done.

There are several general areas where change is possible, any of which can be explored with a person who feels helpless:

- Change patterns of relationships. Identifying and changing behavior that is destructive to lasting relationships can help to mobilize needed support and encouragement from others.
- Change attitudes and outlook. Look at positives that work for good, and see the possibilities along with the problem.
- Change goals and expectations. Realistic goals and expectations help to prevent devastating disappointments.
- Change locations, jobs, friends, or even place of residence. Many painful situations can be avoided by moving away from the circumstances which caused the crisis. This is a drastic form of change and should be weighed carefully before such action is taken.

In order to give up a victim pattern, people will need a good bit of encouragement and assistance. The first step is recognizing that something can be done to bring about a positive change. To make a major change will require time and patient effort on their part, but as they take greater responsibility for their own life, your support can help sustain their progress.

JESUS AND A VICTIM

Sometime later, Jesus went up to Jerusalem for a feast of the Jews. Now there is in Jerusalem near the Sheep Gate a pool, which in Aramaic is called Bethesda and which is surrounded by five covered colonnades. Here a great number of disabled people used to lie—the blind, the lame, the paralyzed. One who was there had been an invalid for thirty-eight years. When Jesus saw him lying there and learned that he had been in this condition for a long time, he asked him, "Do you want to get well?"

"Sir," the invalid replied, "I have no one to help me into the pool when the water is stirred. While I am trying to get in, someone else goes down ahead of me."

Then Jesus said to him, "Get up! Pick up your mat and walk."

(John 5:1–8)

The man by the pool of Bethesda had adapted himself to the role of a victim. Notice especially Jesus' straightforward question "Do you want to get well?" The man's answer focused on his circumstances, but again Jesus focused on the personal desires of the man. He then called for the man to take action for himself; the healing took place as the man stood up, picked up his mat, and walked!

Since we do not have Jesus' authority, most of the healing we see will take months or even years to take place.

By your presence and encouragement, you too can bring that healing into the lives of people who have given up. God's love and power are available through you to bring people the help they need when they have given up believing that they can make any difference in their own lives. Your belief in them can make an important difference.

ANNOTATED BIBLIOGRAPHY

Detweiler-Zapp, Diane, and William Caveness Dixon. *Lay Caregiving*. Philadelphia: Fortress Press, 1982. A good reference for the basics of training lay people for a ministry of caring.

Haugk, Kenneth C. *Christian Caregiving—A Way of Life*. Minneapolis: Augsburg Publishing House, 1984. A practical manual outlining 18 ways Christians can be distinctive in their caring and relating. A resource for pastors, pastoral counselors, and laity. Kenneth C. Haugk is the founder and Executive Director of Stephen Ministries, 1325 Boland, St. Louis, MO 63117.

Hiltner, Seward. *Preface To Pastoral Theology*. Nashville: Abingdon Press, 1958. A classic and foundational study of the nature and style of pastoral care.

Jackson, Edgar. *When Someone Dies*. Philadelphia: Fortress Press, 1971. A concise and practical work on the impact of death and ways of coping with loss.

Kelsey, Morton T. *Caring*. New York: Paulist Press, 1981. An in-depth examination of the many facets of New Testament love and its practical application in various relationships. Kelsey incorporates the insights of Jungian psychology with the biblical perspective on love.

Kinlaw, Dennis. *Helping Skills For Human Resource Development*. San Diego: University Associates, Inc., 1981. A practical and detailed manual for developing the interpersonal skills needed to help another person. Exercises and tapes are included to provide material for specific training experiences.

Kübler-Ross, Elisabeth. *On Death and Dying.* New York: Macmillan Publishing Co., 1969. A landmark work, sensitively written, on the stages of death and grief.

Nouwen, Henri J. *The Wounded Healer.* Garden City, N.Y.: Doubleday & Co., 1972. A strong case is made here for entering personally into the wounded condition of another person in order to become a source of healing.

Nouwen, Henri J. *The Living Reminder.* New York: Seabury Press, 1977. Three addresses to pastors on the importance of cultivating the spiritual life in order to be a living reminder of Jesus Christ.

Oates, Wayne E. *Pastoral Care and Counseling in Grief and Separation.* Philadelphia: Fortress Press, 1976. An insightful analysis of the many facets and types of grief, and helpful suggestions for ministering to the grief-stricken.

Oates, Wayne E. *Your Particular Grief.* Philadelphia: Westminster Press, 1981. A personal and sensitive treatment of the experiences of bereavement and the range of feelings that accompany it.

Powell, John. *Why Am I Afraid To Tell You Who I Am.* Niles, Ill.: Argus Communications, 1969. A down-to-earth treatment of the dynamics of human emotions and relationships.

Southard, Samuel. *Training Church Members For Pastoral Care.* Valley Forge, Pa.: Judson Press, 1982. A description of a training program at the local church level.

Welch, Reuben. *We Really Do Need To Listen.* Nashville: Impact Books, 1971. Reflections on John 13—17 provide the basis for drawing upon God's presence in order to care deeply for one another.

Wise, Carroll A. *The Meaning of Pastoral Care.* New York: Harper & Row, 1966. A very clear and readable introduction to the practice of pastoral care.